LIVING
A JOYOUS LIFE
Practical Spirituality

ELIZABETH JOY

Illustrations: Ashisha
Book Design: Elizabeth Joy
Typography: Pioneer Graphics

JOY is love expressed. The leaves turning colors, season after season. The stars at night. The smile of a loved one. All miracles. We, as humans, are beings of nature clothed in our own self-spun complexities. But in truth, we are beings of pure joy, of beauty and of spirit. And if we surrender to the immense Love that surrounds us constantly, we cannot help but open up our hearts and lend our wisdom to each other. Support each other. Laugh together. We are the Lights of the world.

I believe we have a responsibility to ourselves, to those we love and to all beings on our beloved earth. Our responsibility is to rejoice, to dance, and to love with the Light of joy! God Bless you.

Elizabeth Joy

This book is dedicated to the inspirers, the artists, the musicians, the poets, the visionaries and the lovers of beauty who have kept the flame alive, and to that part within each one of us that holds these timeless gifts.

CONTENTS

CHAPTER ONE
THE OPEN HEART

Whatever is yours by Divine Right will come into your life.

There is an absolute universal truth that says positive belief in yourself and in your Divinity generates love, harmony and joy.

Celebrate yourself and your Divinity! Your inner harmonious vibrations will resonate with peace.

You will be uplifted when you no longer put out negative beliefs which have a weight and create what they affirm. Your beliefs in lack and limitation affirm them.

Positive words and thoughts are much more powerful than negative ones. Affirm the truth of who

3

you are! "I am Divine. I am limitless, infinite, eternal, universal and whole. I am Peace and I am Light." Your entire being resonates to truth! Your path will unfold before you, showing you a world of joy, expansiveness and Divine freedom. Open the doors, and flood your life with peace!

As each day passes, acknowledge the Light you've opened to and the accomplishments you've achieved.

The way to handle any feelings of lack, pain, depression or withdrawal that will allow you to move out of them is to realize that you do have a choice — you can let these energies have expression in your being or you can choose to recognize them and let them go.

It is your reactions to people and situations that determines the quality of your experience. Affirm the positive in the people and situations in your life without dwelling upon or replaying the negative in your heart and mind.

You are free to choose how you react to and view all situations.

Allow positive, loving energy to flow out of you with grace, ease, and joy! Choose the energies that most nurture and soothe you.

Allow your heart to remain open, even in the face of pain or depression when you are most apt to close your heart, pull in your energy and withdraw. This closing and withdrawal increases your pain. It makes it very difficult for the stuck energy to move. In remaining open, you allow the energy to move through you as you watch it come and go, rise and fall, ebb and flow. You and everybody else have felt pain and have lived through it. If you do not create fear about being hurt or feeling pain, much of your hurt and pain will dissipate. The fear of pain is often worse than the pain itself! When pain arises, identify it and do not hold onto it. Let it go.

Let your physical or emotional hurts flow out of your body. Breathe deeply. Call upon your innate sense that all things pass. Tap your inner knowledge that you are beautiful and unique at all times, even in the face of pain.

Expand!

What happens when you close yourself off to pain is that you also close yourself off to life! When you are closed, those things that feel "bad" or those things that feel good cannot move through you! When you are afraid of being hurt what often happens is you shut yourself off from any deep relationship with another being. Vulnerability is a quality of the soul. It is a quality that says, "life happens, and I will be here to taste every drop, my pains, my sorrows, and my joys, because I am expansive enough to encompass it ALL."

One of the greatest emotional pains on earth comes from the disappointment set up by expecting others to love, fill, and make you complete. Until you take the responsibility for yourself, you will not feel fulfilled. Human ego love comes and goes. It accepts and rejects. Do not expect human ego love to fulfill you. It is the permanent Divine Love moving through all that will make you filled.

Perhaps you have tried to manipulate other people to love you. That is not their responsibility. Their responsibility is truly to love themselves. The amazing thing is that when they do, they will love you too. They will express love in all that they do, because they will be love in action — fulfilled and open, beautiful beings. Your job is to love yourself.

*From loving yourself
comes the inner sensitivity
that KNOWS you are loved
and moved by a Divine power
so warm and wondrous.*

When you know that, you are Love, you are warmth, you are Light. At that point you radiate a joy and fullness so beautiful and you are very, very close to Home.

Feel the warmth of your heart center, call upon the vast energy and power and truth of love and allow it to expand through you to embrace and include all.

*You are capable of
loving at every moment.*

Love the joy and the sorrow. Love it and bless it all, for it is all part of the Source, part of the wondrous, empowered movement of life. Keep the softness of an open heart. Let your soul guide you in keeping the love moving through you.

If another does someting to cause you pain, realize that they too are in pain, and what they need is love and support, rather than for you to withdraw your love. Heal them with an open heart by embracing what is going on. And out of the power, softness and wisdom of your being, hold them in the Light. Shine your Light so that you do not take on their pain and close off.

The way out of pain is through the love of the open heart.

If someone acts unkindly, selfishly or withholds their love from you, this is a cry for love, a reflection of the fact that in that moment, they do not love themselves, but are feeling afraid. What they truly need is total forgiveness and support. Be the healer and the giver in the face of pain. It is very easy to be defensive in the face of pain, to want to lash out at someone who has triggered anger or hurt within you.

Know that when you feel someone else has hurt you, you are giving your power away. You DO have a choice — to react with hurt or to embrace yourself and the other with love. The truth is that no one can upset you, unless you already hold the upset inside of you. They trigger it, but it was there to begin with or you would not react by feeling hurt or insulted. Be humble. Learn not to be offended. Realize that the other did not mean to hurt you, but did not know how to communicate or handle their fears, or their pain.

Two people who have the same experience could generate very different reactions. It is up to you.

Choose joy!

If you feel an initial response of pain, take a moment, breathe deeply and open your heart. Know it is at this point that you hold the key to transformation. Send love to whomever may have seemed to trigger pain within you. Thank them for showing you an area that needed your love and attention.

You may have grown up with situations where people would close their hearts or withdraw love from you if you did not please them. This behavior is a reflection of their own unhappiness and lack of self love. Know that you can now choose to react differently. You know the old ways of reacting and being defensive which bring limitation. Take a chance and open up your heart. You will find that the need to have everyone behave in a certain way will fade. You will let others be who they choose to be and you will feel more alive! You will not need others to conform to your needs. You will have so much free energy and will want others to fulfill their own needs, doing what is best for them. That is Love in action.

A true being of love and power is one that makes you feel good about yourself.

A powerful person is a loving person who makes you feel peaceful and at ease, one who cares about and gets along with other people. A powerful person is a humble and gentle person. Their qualities will shine through their eyes, their touch, their words. If you know people who must tell you of their accomplishments, who exaggerate good times or bad, who make you feel less about yourself, you can know they are unhappy within and you can let your Light, understanding and compassion flow to them to heal and uplift.

You are a Light source with the ability to expand everyday into more joy and freedom.

What lies inside of you is as vast as the heavens and the universe beyond. You have believed yourself to be your thoughts, your feelings, your body. This is but a fraction of your totality.

You are a beautiful child of the Light. Rejoice in the spirituality of your own being.

Spirituality is love. It is simple, not always easy because love has been so misunderstood. It has been mistaken to be attachment and dependency. But when these things fall after they rise, there remains something much vaster, much deeper — the love of the soul.

The soul trusts that all is working itself out in just the right way. The soul lets go and lets a greater Divine order move in.

*The love of the soul
is everlasting and timeless.*

It is not there one moment and gone the next.
Spirituality is your very nature. You cannot be separate from it. Spirit breathes life into form. It is a
magnificent, amazing, awe-inspiring creation that
you have decided to participate in, learn from and
grow with. Just as every cell in your body works with
a single purpose, so do human beings, animals, plants
and minerals work together with a single purpose — to
cultivate and nurture your Divinity, the Divinity
within all beings and your connectedness to all
beings. You have gathered in this amazing garden to
know the Vastness in this beautiful disguise just as
you knew it before you separated into individual
form.

*The greatest question you
can live the answer to is how
to be filled by Divine Love
and let it move you
every moment of your life.*

Once you are full, you cannot help but share. You cannot help but be moved by the power. This individuation of Spirit is a lovely, intricate and playful experience and experiment to be savored and enjoyed in humble gratefulness. For in the midst of all of your physicalness, there exists an animating, permeating power and energy. Every single atom on this planet, in the universe and beyond is a part of this energy.

Each being is part of and carries with it the Infinite and Spiritual Light Source.

You have at your disposal a vast amount of creative energy that you can direct in any way that you choose. You are surrounded and enlivened by a constant, churning, vital energy. There is no where this energy is not. Sparkling, radiant, clear, forever, shining for all — the power, energy and Love of the Divine. Feel it moving through you to touch all other beings.

The river flows into itself,
an endless stream
of beauty, grace and joy.

CHAPTER TWO
LIGHT OF YOUR SOUL

God is limitless.
You are a part of God
and you are limitless.

Your soul is your Godself. Your soul is that part of you that is in touch with your essence. Allowing your soul to guide you opens doors of healing, harmonious relationships and positive situations.

True masters are in a constant state of surrender to their higher Godself. When you perceive through the open heart, you touch your soul, with full compassion for the Godself in every being. Your soul knows all of the possibilities that are best for you, and you can become in touch with these possibilities by quieting your mind and opening your heart.

When you quiet your being, you will receive certain impressions, certain feelings, visualizations or sounds or fragrances. When you have connected to your soul the information you receive will guide you toward freedom, peace and love.

Your soul is the voice of Love.
Is is the voice of Light
and inner freedom.

Your Godself feels soothing and calm and communicates to you in a very soft, compassionate way. If you have an expansive and loving view of a person, idea or situation, where before you did not, that is the perception of your higher Godself. The higher Godself sees the unity in all things. It is the voice that says "I see the love, the common thread between all beings — the essence."

Your ego will look for differences. Your ego is the voice of confusion that believes you are separate from all others and that you must fight for your needs, your identity and your security. Your ego seeks to exclude. Your soul is always expanding and including. When your ego has a hold on you, breathe deeply and accept responsibility for your feelings and actions and your soul will shine through.

*Your soul feels your
connection to all others and
all forms and facets of nature.*

Forgive yourself for acting from your ego. How many times have you had the opportunity to act with the grace of your soul and instead got angry? To move past this behavior, identify what you really want, what is hurting so much that your system cries out. What you usually want is love, security, perfection. One of the most important lessons in your life, is taking responsibility for your own love, your own security and your own sense of perfection. Your soul will show you the ways to take responsibility, moment by moment.

*All that is, right now,
is perfect for this moment.*

Many are opening to feelings of connectedness, of the Light of their soul. There is no separation. There is one Divine mind. Your soul is the channel to Divine mind.

Feel the pure golden Light shining within you.

Many times your soul will bring you information through your body. Try this exercise when you are making a decision. Bring a few options into your consciousness. Pay attention to how your body feels when you think of the first option. If your body feels light and easy, then this is your soul's way of letting you know that this option would bring you the most peace and light. If your body feels heavy or your throat or stomach feel tight, this is your soul letting you know that as the circumstances exist now, this option would bring you less freedom and less peace. See which option feels the lightest and freest. This is one of the most direct ways your soul has of communicating with you.

All that you do is movement toward higher awareness, though it may seem at times that it is not.

The illusion is that what you see is all that exists.

Your soul is in touch with that which is beyond illusion, with the energies behind all forms.

Why have we as a consciousness for thousands of years, forsaken the higher aspect of our being? If we are so potentially evolved, and our essence is Light and love, then why have we chosen to live with the ego? What we learned by the ego self leading our consciousness is that we can never be fulfilled by it. The world of materialism will never truly satisfy. We now know this to the fullest, so that we are seeking the truth, the strength and the Light of who we truly are. Your soul has always known that the way to be a filled, loving being is to seek within and know your higher Godself.

It is infinitely beautiful
when you make the choice
to see with the healing
Light of your soul.

Your soul sees the world as a very friendly place to live. It brings you towards more healing, towards more Light, more aliveness, more creativity and towards more love and your strength shines through like a diamond. There will always be the perfect experiences for you. When you move through them with grace and ease, you lend this graceful energy to the next person. There will always be help and guidance, if you ask for it, and listen. The more that you act on what is given, the more that will come.

The following are some affirmations for bringing in your soul self, and transforming your world into a place of light, joy, laughter and love. Use these or create your own to affirm the truth of who you are — a Divine, radiant soul!

My Essence is Love.

I am One with all.

I Surrender to this Moment.

I Generate Peace and Harmony.

I am Inspired and Creative.

I am a Healing Source.

I Listen to others with an Open Heart.

I am a Source of Light.

My Love is Limitless.

Whatever I Give out Flows Back to Me.

I am Beautiful.

I am Valuable.

I am Spirit on Earth.

I am Love.

CHAPTER THREE
CELEBRATE YOURSELF!

*When you have the constant
focus of going within and
then acting, your life will
unfold in magical ways.*

Those things that are no longer necessary will fall away, and in their place more light and joy will come. Joy, peace, love, courage, strength, humour and all soul qualities are energies which have their own movement and their own dance; they will join with you the moment you make space for them in your being. When you allow these qualities to move through you, you become the grounding force for them.

In order to be fluid and move with grace through all situations, make space inside of you. You can feel when you are blocked. It feels heavy, on your feet or in your heart and mind. When you allow space to be within you, you are flexible, light and free.

Make the conscious choice to receive your own enlightenment — being light in mind, body and spirit.

All that you are right now is wondrous, magical, Divine and beautiful.

Let your smile convey the energy of your heart. Let wisdom twinkle in your eyes and move forth from you. You extend this energy to all others to feel and to use, whether you connect with them physically or not. When you feel good and light, this emanates far from you to touch all others and you will attract magic and joy into your life in the perfect forms and energies for you.

As you embody Love, you are the endless receiver of its gifts.

CELEBRATE YOURSELF!

Connect with yourself — your depths. Sit and listen with no expectations of hearing something specific. Be open to what your Light has to say to you. Your Light does have something to say to you. It will gladly and lovingly carry you everywhere. Your inner voice, your connected self has information, feeling tones, direction, and energy available to you at all times. Out of your centered awareness, out of your Light, in response to whatever is taking place, will come the Divine choice, the right move, the joy-filled moment. You have never been separate from the One Spiritual Source.

The Source is vaster than the stars and all the sky. It is in the trees, in the bird's feathers, in the wash of the shore, in the eyes of another. It is what you are. Touch your inner awareness — your personal touchstone of the heart — to guide you in your outer awareness.

Being spiritual simply means that you answer your own questions.

You make your own choices and you take responsibility for them. Some will recognize your Light, and some may not because they need to play out a different pattern. Let it be.

---

*Feeling Love in your heart
is the strongest way you have of
affecting change on the planet.*

Leave everyone to their own destiny. Observe clearly, without judgement, without straining your perceptions through the eyes of the past.

Love yourself, including your past and your growth, for your past created your life today. Be grateful for what you have learned, for all that you are aware of and for your sensitivity.

Gratitude is a Divine energy. It is a healer. The more time you can spend in a state of gratitude, the more at peace and fulfilled you will feel. When you feel grateful for the positive things in your life, you let the universe know that you are willing to receive more and give more and Love more and channel your energy toward the good of all. This brings the greatest blessings.

Concentrate your energy on the positive things in your life and you will attract more positive energy to you. What you focus on, increases.

Look upon each situation with new eyes, with aliveness and with joy!

Let your emotions flow through you and go back home to love. Do not be attached to those things which you believe have made you feel happy or sad. Your soul, in a particular chosen vehicle, comes to earth for the exact length of time and the exact experiences it needs to grow, to share its light and ultimately, to Love. Your essence is Love.

There is in truth, no positive and no negative. There is no absolute right or wrong. There is only energy and you choose how you view a specific situation, person or idea. The beauty of each moment is that it brings with it its own set of circumstances and therefore what is appropriate one moment will not be the next and vice-versa. Your job is to ride the wave of the moment. Remember the path of least resistance. Life needn't be an endless struggle, if you follow the signs from your inner self. Where the signs point, is where your connected self is showing you the way.

Walk through the open doors. Ride the wave of the moment.

A moment ago, the "sign" said turn left, and now you are seeing another sign and it says stay where you are. Your job is to follow the signs, moment by moment. The signs from yesterday or one hour ago are not necessarily today's signs and thank goodness for the imploding, exploding wonder of change and spontaneity! Your job is to follow the signs. They are there!

Do not get so caught up in concepts that you forget to experience life as it happens in front of you! You are never given anything you are not ready for. You are always at the right place at the right time. The patterns and energies in your life are not random. What moves into your life, as well as what moves out of your life does so with good reason. Allow this inherent perfection of movement.

If you remain rigid in the face of change, you will snap. If you remain flexible and humble, you will arrive very peacefully and enjoyably on the other side of the shore, having crossed the river of change with grace and ease, and even having had time for lunch on the way. Calm your energy in the face of change and take it one step at a time.

Your life is unfolding in just the way it is meant to.

You cannot know what the future brings, because the moment you are in the future, it is the present, So, enjoy!

The intensity of any feeling will move on. So even your sorrow, which may seem at times to be overwhelming, does have its own cycle. If you observe it, sit with it, watch it, feel it, love it and allow it to be, it will move on. Much of the problem lies in the fact that one spends much time trying to cover, get rid of, ignore or suppress sorrow, that an even bigger blockage than one began with is created. Let yourself be free to flow and transform naturally.

Watch the things you give your time and energy to. Move yourself out of things that are not making you feel one hundred percent alive, vibrant and joyous.

Life is meant to be embraced, revered and celebrated by all of your thoughts, acts and words.

No need to give energy to negative images of your-self as this perpetuates them. Feed yourself with positive acceptance, and you will find others looking at you in the same way. The wonderful irony is that when you know in your heart what you believe in, you won't need outside approval for those beliefs. You will not feel threatened if others have different beliefs than you do.

Be a very good friend to yourself.

It is the number one way you have of being a friend to others. When you are joyful, you will be a joy to be around. When you are loving, you will find love coming back at you. When you are centered and balanced, you will draw to you centered and balanced situations and people. Be the first to act out of love. Your world will open up before your eyes. One man or woman's world can be bleak and dull, and the next man or woman's world can be warm and fulfilling. It has to do with the way you choose to react to the many circumstances you encounter each day.

CELEBRATE YOURSELF!

Find your safety, warmth and expansiveness by knowing that Life is a celebration of your divinity, freedom, and spontaneity within! Each moment is newborn — filled with delight and wonder.

You are beautiful just the way you are.

You are a perfect reflection of Spirit, of the Divine, of Source.

Call it what you will, it remains elusively nameless and faceless, until you look into the mirror and see it looking back at you! You are that force, expressed. So love it, and love with it, for you are that. Peace.

CHAPTER FOUR
BEAUTIFUL
RELATIONSHIPS

There is always a relationship in your life — with another person, with God, with nature, with an animal — grow into another and you will know — it is all part of the One.

Your personal preferences are unique to you. You feel comfortable with some situations and not with others. Spend time enjoying yourself and learning what these preferences are. Respect and truly nurture yourself. Affirm yourself! "I am me, and I am beautiful and I am radiant!"

Do the things that bring you joy, healing and aliveness!

For in doing them, you create more joy, healing and aliveness.

In relationship with another, express yourself. Let the other know who you are. Communicate. Share your beautiful self. You needn't be afraid of expressing yourself or of allowing the other to do so. When you commit your energy to being with someone, communicate what your needs and preferences are. Create open, honest situations where each person can express themselves and be heard, trusted, respected, understood and accepted by the other. Hear, trust, respect, understand and accept yourself.

Support others in expressing themselves, creatively, wholly and comfortably.

Remember not to judge their needs or your own. When you are fulfilled and whole within and expressing yourself, you will attract others who are whole and who are capable of expressing their wholeness.

When you draw to you another being whom you deeply love, realize that you love them because of exactly who they are. You love them because of their unique preferences and totality, and ALLOW this beautiful totality. They are a unique being. It is essential to accept the other person just as they are without wanting to change or control them. Who they are is who you were attracted to in the first place! You do not need to live with them, but they are entitled to be themselves.

Open communication and open hearts are the basis of all beautiful relationships.

When you do not have expectations of a person to behave in a certain way, you will not set up frustrations or disappointments.

It is important that if compromises need to be made, both people feel comfortable with them. View the

41

other with compassion. One way to objectively look at situations in relationships is to look at the situation as if you were another person. For a moment, step back. View yourself as if you were a friend of yours! What could you do that would bring the most Light and love to the situation? Oftentimes, you see what will bring the most Light and love, but feel inhibited from acting upon it. If you view yourself objectively for a few moments, you can imagine yourself acting in the most compassionate way. You can see yourself playing out the most loving, forgiving option, and can visualize the situation completed with joy and the other person and yourself feeling at peace. It can be helpful to bring other people into your consciousness and speak with them telepathically. Tell the other what is in your heart, and let them know that you support them. Making this telepathic rapport before actually talking with them can help clear up the energy and set up positive vibrations between you.

You choose how you will react in all relationships, with all people.

See the parts of yourself that feel hurt or rejected. Nurture them and show them that you care. Take those parts of you that react emotionally and let them know you are there for them. See them in a clear light. Know that they are not you, in your wholeness, but a small part, or voice within you that is from your past. Show them that the present is free, and different, expansive and healed. Show them your wholeness. Uplift them with love.

The reason parts of you may feel hurt or rejected is because you have expected the outside world to give you something that you did not realize you can give to yourself.

The moment you desire security from another, you create them as your authority — you give away your power.

You will find security in the outer world the moment you feel secure inside.

Keep your heart open, ask within and you will know for you what is appropriate for you at every moment with each relationship you encounter. You will know! Shine your Light! There are no rules. Just be aware and alive, moment by moment by moment and your Light will shine through to all areas of your life. Follow your signs! Express who you truly are and allow the other person their wholeness. Rejoice in the everchanging facets of love, life and power that you are both reflecting. Energies are moving between you constantly.

---

*Choose to express
the Light and you cannot
be other than loving*

You may not always agree with another, but allow them their ISNESS, and express yours as well.

---

*The times you are not in
agreement with another, you
will be asked by your deep
self to remain loving and
continue to expand your energy.*

BEAUTIFUL RELATIONSHIPS

You can always choose to leave or change a situation, but to do so with love is the most healing, beautiful way. You know what brings the most growth, the most love and most joy into your life — act accordingly.

If a particular relationship is meant to be, it shall be. But to force a square peg into a round hole is not natural. To force a situation that does not feel natural will usually result in an uncomfortable, painful situation. Know that the more you tune in to the inner realms, your inner wisdom, the more you will listen to and follow your inner guidance, and with guidance will come the way to love and those beings that resonate with your energy. And when you truly are loving, you will draw to you your own.

Any relationship is as loving as the two individuals are loving.

Your greatest joy will unfold when you are willing to allow it.

To love another is truly to put their well being before your own and with this kind of love comes deep blessings.

When you can be yourself and hold the other person in your heart with love, you can go anywhere. You have the Light on your side. You cannot love without the Light. So keep on loving again and again and again.

Follow your heart.

Understand that what soul mate is about, is feeling that the other person is more important than your own being, because you are one and the same being, you have been together and known each other. The understanding is so great, that in the end it is their life you value more than your own. The cosmic joke is that all life is one anyway, so you have taken this truth and presented it to another whom you love deeply; you have said, I know you, I love you, and you are me.

When you choose to Love,
you can never be
separate from anyone.

BEAUTIFUL RELATIONSHIPS

You can never lose anyone or anything if you go on loving. Because it is through love that you are connected to all beings, all energies, whether they are on the earth plane or not. Those who have made a transition and gone beyond the earth plane, can STILL LOVE and STILL RECEIVE LOVE BACK.

Please open to this truth and just continue to Love! For in loving, you are the Light.

You are connected to everyone you have ever truly Loved, as you cannot be separate from that which you Love.

CHAPTER FIVE
FEEL THE SPARK

The truth is
there is only this moment.

You have a past with memories of certain experiences and you often carry them with you, coloring the present moment. Your present moment becomes filtered through the perceptions and conditionings of your past. And how sad this is, to lose the present moment to yesterday. Total and complete participation in the moment brings inner freedom, a true present and joy!

The past is kept alive by memory, the future by hopes or fears. To live with your total being in the moment needs all of your attention. As you meet people or look at yourself and the world, the way to freedom is to perceive without judgement, without comparison and without opinions of how things SHOULD be! Just enjoy and celebrate the uniqueness of each individual and each moment!

Conflict arises from having an idea of the way things SHOULD be while not accepting what IS.

Change is possible when you are aware of what is. Crystal clear perception of what is before you is the very key to its transformation. Out of clear seeing comes clear action and all things beautiful. The seeing and acting become one. Fluidity. Flow. Movement. Rhythm.

Often times you will think, compare and weigh and then make a mental decision, based upon your past conditioning, rather than out of the vast beauty, endless power and aliveness of the present moment. When you are unsure of how to act and weigh a decision over and over, let it go for a while. Rest. If you had the correct decision you would not be weighing it against another one over and over — you would know. Wait for the knowing. Then move with grace. Right action is immediate and natural when you are aware of what is before you — when you are living fully in the moment.

Looking for answers prevents acting, it prevents being, because you are not being, you are looking and you miss the moment! The "answers" lie in direct perception of the moment. The freedom you seek lies in total and complete perception of what is.

As each moment unfolds its gifts, you have infinite opportunities to feel joy and love. The inner flame dances into Light.

When you see exactly what is before you with all its energy, all of its churning, wondrous power, without the desire to change, compare, judge or qualify, you begin to see the energy beyond form, the essence beyond manifestation. You are in the present, with all of its newness, openness and aliveness. You begin to hear beyond words and move into a space of magical wonder and joy.

Inherent within the present moment is the infinite wisdom to guide you discerningly and lovingly.

A truly free and aware mind is free from all constraints, fears, grudges and opinions; free to see the present situation in a clear light. Free to open your arms to embrace the moment. Compassion, deep sensitivity and awareness naturally arise when you live in the moment. Don't carry your past around with you like a sack of potatoes on your back. Bringing the past into the present distorts your ability to see. You have a friend and have created an image of who they are and of who you want them to be, an image of them based upon what they did last week, last year and so on. They too have an image of you. These images are in relationship to each other! Perceiving through images prevents you from having actual relationships. All images block true perception. In clear seeing, the image creating stops. Clear seeing is love.

See the other person as they truly are without wanting to change them. When you desire external forces, such as another person to change in order to make you happy, they cannot possibly make you happy! If you are unfulfilled, another person changing will not fill you! They are expressing their divinity, their totality in a very perfect way for them. When you see them through your images you block yourself from seeing their true Divinity, their Cosmic Self — aware of its meaning at every moment. Allow them their space, their dance, their beingness. Allow them to choose, to grow, to live as they are. Love them. Give them support and faith. They are not now who they were yesterday, or five years ago. They are growing, changing, and shifting and so are you.

The greatest gift you can give to another is clear perception of them without judgement, opinion or comparison, much like watching a waterfall.

You will hear the silence of the being you are with. You will hear beyond the words, into the totality and the essential expression of the other. This is true meditation. Meditation is not the mental repetition of a word of phrase. That is not meditation. And if you are not a loving being before you began repeating this word or phrase, you will not be loving afterwards.

As a divine being, your job is to tap your inner wisdom and love, and use it on the earth plane.

Each moment, you are called upon by the Infinite Spirit, within your being, to be loving and wise and beautiful. Therein lies the purpose of coming to earth.

Live life for yourself and not through someone else's eyes. See yourself and the world around you through your own shining eyes! There is no one who has greater authority for yourself, than you do. If someone tells you otherwise, they have created a need in themselves to be filled by something outside of themselves!

*To truly help another,
increase their sense of
self-worth, self love
and self-appreciation.*

The more they appreciate themselves, the less they will make something outside of themselves their authority. You are a special unique human being. Your gift to the world is you! Share that gift.

*Keep the Light in your heart,
rather than the passing values
of the material world.*

What can you do for others? How can you help another? The Great Ones, the Masters and Servants of Light have always come with that question in their hearts. How can I help another? How can I transmute some of the negativity surrounding them and let them move on to a lighter state? And you too have this job! You will always be taken care of by the One Source. Be concerned with what you can give to others. You are all One.

The ether, the space between you and other beings is filled with churning, vital, alive energy. The space between you connects you to all other beings. It is filled with love, with power and with movement. You are not separate! The darkness and the light contained in all other beings is a reflection of the darkness and the light contained within you. All voices are your voice. You may not have touched a certain part within yourself. You may not recognize a voice as your own, but the deeper you see, the more that you go within, the more famliar every single voice in the universe will sound. All sorrows are your sorrow. All joys are your joy.

Arise to the wonder; surrender to the goodness and grace of each timeless moment.

When your whole being gets quiet, it will sing a different tune. You will be the holder of the key, the owner of silence. You will KNOW without a doubt that you are Spirit in action. You will know that your life is unfolding in magical and perfect ways. You will sense a harmony greater than one you could imagine and yet you are an integral part of this harmony.

You are the song of the Divine.

You are the song of the Divine, just as much as the birds are the song, as much as the waves crashing against the shore are the song.

Within this totally new rhythm, you will be free; free to listen within and know you are God, know you are joy. As you accept your inherent perfection, so shall you return home, so shall you be a being of heaven on the winds of eternity. There is so much love for you, so much support coming from other people, other realms, other dimensions. There is so much joy at your awakening. You are so very dearly loved. Realize and rejoice in your wholeness. Your consciousness determines your experience. YOU guide your consciousness.

*When you are free
you give your wholeness to
this earth — making the
flowers bloom, the birds soar
and humans Love.*

Your lightness, or enlightenment lives in the now.
You have all, now — no past projections onto the pres-
ent, no future hopes or fears distorting the moment.
Love lives in the present moment.

*The everrunning waters of life
flow through the now.*

With the very perception of what is, comes love.
Goodness enters your heart and the innocence of
kindness arises. The rhythm of the moment becomes
your rhythm. Your movement becomes as a flower
reaching out its petals towards the sky, filled with a
naturalness and an insight into this entire movement

of life with all of its sorrow, joy and desires. You are free to move beyond thought, beyond your acquired knowledge, into something much greater, into something nameless, timeless and immeasurable. In that energy, lies the Source of all.

Feel the spark,
and the flame will burn.

CHAPTER SIX
INNER SENSITIVITY

Each being is a magnificent forcefield of color, tone, beauty and vibration.

Your physical body is surrounded and permeated by a pure energy body, the aura, that emanates light and has movements of energy moving through, around, away from and towards it. You are made of energy and it is to energy that you shall return. You can place your hands or direct your healing energy to any point on your body that needs some extra care. You can send energy anywhere you may need light and healing and you will feel warmth and flow. Know that you ARE energy.

Relax.

Just let the energy flow. Healing is an inherent gift within you, and it begins to unfold when you FEEL loving. You begin to feel loving when you realize that it is YOU that must generate love in your life. When you are the generator of love, your expectations for things to work out in a particular way fade. You hold the Light and then you are whole.

When you touch healing, you are touching Love.

When you relax into gratitude and wonderful acceptance of yourself and this world, you will know yourself as a natural channel of healing light.

Receive. Receptivity is a way of being. It is healing quality of the soul. Receive the person you are with, the grass under your feet, the energies surrounding you, a cup of tea, love, a smile. How much are you willing to receive? Simply sit with yourself and generate receptivity. Take in the earth, the sky, your home, your children. Just receive. No expectations.

When you bring a person, situation or idea into your consciousness, what kind of energy comes with it? What is the feeling surrounding it? Heavy and dense? Light and playful? Joyous, sad? Blocked, open? Be aware of the energy and you will tune into more than what the physical senses perceive. You pick up energy all of the time. It is natural.

Before you took on a body, your perceptions were not limited to the senses and they still are not.

You communicate telepathically with all beings. When you are aware of this, you can choose which energies you will take in, and which energies you will not.

The more centered you are, the stronger you feel, the less affected you will be by other people's energies. When you are centered and strong, you send this out telepathically and others receive it and are lifted. Feel good and you will create good. Await the positive with open arms knowing that you are Spirit in action. Positive expectation brings positive situations to you, not always the way you might have envisioned them.

You are creating your life with the power and magic of the Infinite Source.

Whatever is yours by divine right, you cannot lose. If something is not divinely yours, you do not want it, as it will not bring your highest and most joyous good.

When you step aside and allow Spirit to guide the situations in your life, Divine order is truly yours and the blessings will flow. You can turn any situation around by turning your attitudes around, seeing the highest good in all that you create. Your faith is your guiding light. Let it shine!

Dedicate yourself to living a joyous life!

If you feel joyous, loving, warm and abundant, you will draw that to you. With a positive expectation, you will draw to you your highest good. It is more than a mental visualization. It is a very real feeling that becomes a part of you. Ask yourself what kinds of things you feel will happen to you. Your answer will show you why certain things come your way. If you feel a black cat brings bad luck, and a four-leaf clover brings good, so it will be. Save your pennies for a rainy day, and sure enough the drops will start to fall. Your feelings spin into situations. All is energy.

Believe in the universe. Trust it to share with you all that you need to know and feel and experience. Only you can fulfill the role of your perfect divine destiny.

Believe in yourself!

To hear your inner guidance, stand strong as an individual. Keep on higher ground. Move with the grace of an eagle and the finesse of a dolphin. Become as free as a waterfall. Communicate with stillness. Feel yourself peeling away the layers holding you from entering a higher, deeper realm. Know yourself, permeating all space and form, as the Creative Source.

Trust yourself and your sensitivity.

Your intuition is your key, your pathway to the Divine rhythm of the universe, of which you are a vital part.

It is your all-emcompassing voice and pictures within, not the mental voice and pictures. It is immediate, non-wavering, and sure. If you question which voice you are hearing, the mental or the intuitive, let the issue go. When you hear the intuitive and are ready to trust it, you will know. Trusting your inner self is walking through the door to positive situations.

The open door will be the path of least resistance. The doorways will always be there — you make the choice to walk through them.

INNER SENSITIVITY

Pay attention. The natural way to live, move and be in the world involves using your inner knowing, your inner sensitivity. Include this sensitivity, trust it, welcome it home, for in truth, it has never left you. You have simply chosen, at times, to turn your back upon it, upon a very natural part of your True Self.

If you do not receive intuitive understanding about an issue, situation or idea, simply let it go for the time being. Any information that you are meant to have will absolutely be there for you. Any experience you are meant to have will absolutely be there for you. It cannot be otherwise. God does not get wires crossed. See the inherent perfection that lies within you — the rhythm and harmony of every movement of your life.

You are perfection itself — life overflowing.

You cannot figure everything out. Certain things will happen and you can spend endless hours trying to "understand." You cannot possibly understand the events in your life through your intellect because you are so much greater than your intellect. When you perceive through a limited part of yourself, you perceive a limited view. Your intellect is limited. Do not limit yourself to the filtered perception of the intellect. Surrender trying to figure everything out to accepting the blissful state that says, "It happened. I accept it and move on." You are here to experience your life, not to analyze it! Analyzing prevents action.

Beauty is an attribute of God — inner, outer, all pervasive beauty — the truth of who you are.

Beauty is an attribute of God. Visual creations and peaceful surroundings are a very valid path to the Light. The beauty of nature, of artistic expression, of a beautiful being, animal or plant that shines from within — your entire being responds to beauty! What you can see physically has been given more importance than the energy and love emanating from what you see. Beauty is an energy. Look at the flowers that rise from the sidewalk cracks. Observe the sunsets as they meld with celestial color. Feel paint on the end of a brush as it moves across canvas. Hear the tones of an instrument as it is played by one of great depth and feeling. Look into your friend's eyes. Be aware of beauty.

Music absolutely does affect your auric field. You are transformed by the energy being put out by the artists. When you are aware of this you can monitor your personal response. Music is tone, vibration and energy and you are too, and when the tones merge with your aura, there is a distinct change and a definite movement within your field of energy.

You hold the grace
of the Divine within you.

Different environments create different feeling tones and responses within you. Suffice it to say a traffic jam will create a much different energy than a meadow of wildflowers. Please know that you are a sensitive being and be aware of your personal responses. When you are at peace, you extend that peace to the transformation of the earth.

Awaken to that
place in consciousness
that is your peace.

There are things in this life that deeply move you, that you will give your energy to, and there will be things you will pass by. You know what is truly appropriate for you. Move gently into your own words, your own ideas. You are constantly being given other people's words and ideas and opinions. In deep silence, find your own words. Be your beautiful self. When you move into deep silence, this silence will operate even when you are talking or playing. With this silence will come your own words, your own right action and your own integral way of being in the world. Love yourself.

In this moment, you have at your disposal all of the necessary energy, love and wisdom to transform the present moment into one of joy, awareness and peace.

Tap the endless wellspring of joy within you.

Tap the energy. True insight comes when your mind is free — uncluttered with expectations, memories, opinions and judgements. True insight comes when your awareness is totally in the present moment. With this insight comes sheer delight; a way to live in peace, and in harmonious love. Life is meant to be lived, not just pondered about!

INNER SENSITIVITY

God's very nature is joy. When you attune yourself to joy, you feel an infinite beauty arise inside of you. You have an important part in this time of Awakening. With your words, your song, your energy, you affect your world and the world around you. Share your visions, your beauty, your joy!

You are the Light of the world.

CHAPTER SEVEN
THE GARDEN

*There is a timeless part of
you and nature allows you
insight into its existence.*

The world of nature can be experienced in a very empowering way. Nature is a mirror, a reflection of the vast natural beauty that lies within you. A placid lake reflects the depths of your inner self — radiant and clear. The strong and majestic mountains reflect the strength and majesty you hold within. You are more than your thoughts and beliefs. You hold a timeless essence.

The beauty of the natural world is a perfect reflection of your inner soul.

Humans have placed themselves above the other kingdoms on earth and that is an untrue and isolated position. It has caused much imbalance. We have alienated ourselves from the other natural kingdoms; actually, we need their strength, their uniqueness, their beauty and their wisdom. Their love has always been there for us.

Nature is the natural healer. To be cut off from nature is to be cut off from a part of ourselves. To deny yourself a relationship with nature is to deny your natural place among the heavens and the earth. We have much to learn from the other kingdoms. We are all in this beautiful earth plane experience together to share, to rejoice and to love.

*All of the energies —
plant, mineral, animal
and human are essential
to the Createdness that
exists on earth.*

There are also unseen energies that exist in the realm of the earth plane. They have an evolutionary pattern of their own, but work together with the human, animal, plant and mineral kingdoms. These angelic beings of Light and wisdom are ever so near, and often unrecognized. There exists in the energy surrounding you, beings of Light and wisdom who have been with you all of the time, serving, opening doors, assisting, loving and guiding you. The more you can be grateful to these energies, even if you cannot fully perceive or feel them, the more you can participate in your own evolution.

The purpose of coming to this realm to experience physical life is to expand your consciousness and that begins with and ultimately leads to the constant energy of pure Love. There are energies helping you to do this. They do not make decisions for you, or take your lessons away from you. They simply and lovingly look after you, lift you when you are down, cloak you in warmth when you shed tears, and point the way when you need to know.

All you need to do is be grateful for the endless support systems that exist in this beautiful Createdness

---

All facets of nature are totally involved in this grand experiment of life on earth. The more time you can spend outdoors, the more you will attune to her secrets, her power and her knowledge. Nature is a strong and generous force. The more you can be nurtured by the wind and its rhythm, by the trees and their stability, the less alone you will feel. Spend time listening to a stream, to the ongoing waterflow. You will touch the qualities of flow and change, of love and giving, of release and music in your own life. Spend time looking at the sky and its vastness, at the stars, at the clouds and their artistic movement, and you will touch the dance, movement, softness and flow in your own life. Imagine where the birds in flight, soaring through the clouds and beyond, are going and find a sense of adventure and spontaneity in your own life.

THE GARDEN

Watch a wildflower blooming and know that your purpose in life is to be totally yourself, uninhibited, flowing, free.

Each flight you take, each time you "take off" you are touching others, moving forth and expanding. Watch how you touch others. Is it with encouragement, support, love? Through your gestures, smiles, words and energy, you transform their moment.

Add to the positive beliefs people hold in themselves and of the world.

Increase their sense of love and joy! Empower your world. You can send a blessing to anyone in your life. As you do this, the effect is very far-reaching. Part of your contribution to the healing and upliftment of the planet, absolutely can be done in consciousness. Where you focus your consciousness is where the energy goes.

*Do not underestimate
the power of sending out
energy to those in need.*

At this time, there are many in need and many who would greatly benefit from your love and healing energy. Those whom you send energy to may not call you up the next day with a thank you, but they will receive the energy. How they use it is up to that individual and the Light of their soul. You cannot know what is ultimately best for another and they cannot know for you. Each person has an infinite intelligence guiding their major decisions. Each person's path is perfect for them.

*Accept the inherent flow of
each being. Leave everything
to fulfill its own destiny.*

One of the most beautiful and healing things you can do for another and for the planet is to quietly send out energy from your heart to be used in whatever way that is needed.

Send many loving blessings to Mother Earth who breathes, feels and holds you as her own. Send out blessings to the animals, that we may exchange with them in a much more whole way, so that we may realize all of the beauty, all of the goodness and all of the love that they give unconditionally. We are honored to have these special beings in our lives.

The animals that have come to live with you have come for a very special and important interchange of energy.

On a soul level, they are aware of what they have chosen to experience; you must fulfill your responsibility to them. Many times animals are aware of who you are deeply, spiritually, and they may even be aware of what you are going through. They are often intuitives, healers, and always loving friends when treated with the kindness and care that awareness fosters. Take great loving pride in your relations with them. These special beings need love, attention and care, same as all beings. When you bridge the worlds of life forms, you gain great insight into the similarity between all beings. It is then that compassion arises.

There are dimensions other than the earth plane. There is a dimension of color, where your experience consists totally of the vibration and energy of color. You exist in this dimension long enough for your essence to experience color, to understand that each one carries a different and useful energy. You learn by experience how to integrate color into your vibrations, which ones make you feel powerful and alive, which ones soothe you and so on.

*Life is weaving tapestries
of sound and color
into song and visions.*

There are dimensions of sound, where you experience tone and harmony. You come to understand how to take tone and sound into your own vibration, how to integrate sounds, blend with harmony, how certain sound vibrations make you feel and so on. There are many dimensions that you have existed on before coming to earth. You are familiar with music, color, smell and touch because you have experienced them before as you evolved on earth or in other dimensions.

Your energy form has been exactly where it needed to be to evolve fully, insightfully and lovingly to where you are now. Be grateful for all of the wonder that you are participating in!

This time on earth has many healing energies and opportunities to touch your Divinity; your harmonious sense of inner strength, gratitude, serenity and love!

---

*Attune yourself
to the wisdom of nature
and be whole again.*

CHAPTER EIGHT
FOLLOW YOUR HEART

You are a child of the Light
with a wondrous gift
to share with the world.

There are no directions on the "box of enlighten-ment." There is no one particular path to truth. You cannot put rules on the Source. The Divine is much too creative, loving and free to box you — a part of it — in! Each moment brings with it its own fullness, its own inherent set of rules. What is considered right action one moment may be inappropriate the next.

Contained within each question is the answer.

The right action is contained within you. An inherent wisdom lies within you. This wisdom will show you the way, moment by moment by moment. Tapping this wisdom involves trusting that it does exist! It involves risking your limited viewpoint for a much greater one. It involves extending yourself into the warmth of the power that moves you, that gives you breath and makes your heart beat. You are not isolated. You are plugged into a power so warm, so loving, so wise and beautiful. You are comprised of a vast energy field, a swirling, shimmering movement, reaching out high and deep, backward and forward.

Your energy transcends space and time, churning, dancing, and rising up from within you.

FOLLOW YOUR HEART

You are blessed with language and action but your essence is so far beyond that. You are not a body. You have a body. Your body is energy. Your cells respond to positive thoughts and to love.

When you turn your face within, you will be filled with a gratitude and a softness so real and true. Touch the softness and flow inside of yourself. Feel the thaw of any past hurts. Extend Love, for it comes back to you many fold, for healing, for upliftment and for sheer joy!

You are a consciousness, a free spirit, a song of joy.

Release these forces within so simply by realizing them. You are the Light of the world, the everlasting sun, holding a wreath of glittering jewels in your crown of life's magical peace. Radiate forth the new, the sleeping beauty within. Be full of ever-inspired melodies. True to yourself, a dawn of peace. You are unique.

Religions are built around one person's experience of enlightenment. The experience is interpreted, organized, and written about to no end. And then comes the rules — the way that you too can attain what so and so attained, IF you follow the rules! Remember that the rules were not set forth by the one who experienced enlightenment. They were set forth by very average people with a certain degree of political power who said, "let's put things in order so that there are rules and prescriptions everyone should follow so that we can control the people." It is a trap. Your ego has convinced itself that if you follow the rules, then you are somehow good, and you are on your way. If you do not follow the rules, then your ego would love you to believe that you are somehow bad. Do you think Buddha followed the rules? Do you believe that the Christ followed the rules? Perhaps one of the strongest qualities in each of these lives was the great spontaneity, the incredibly vast awareness that enabled them to spontaneously fit their actions exactly to the situation at hand. They did not act according to some tomb of a manuscript they had memorized! They had the power inside of them, as you do, and they claimed it and it moved them and that was the perfection and the harmony that was their lives. This did not mean that they did not ache or feel pain. It meant that they knew it was all part of life, part of the vast power of God, and they surrendered to this, moment after moment after moment. They knew that the power that was moving them would not let them down, it could not possibly let them down, just as it cannot possibly let you down. It is only the ego that disappoints, that limits, that clings to fear.

*The Divine in you surrenders
to the vast beauty of all
that is going on before
it, moment by moment!*

And that is love and God in action! Your enlightenment is already within you.

You are the vastness.

I would suggest to you that at some point, you will
have to live by your own spontaneity, following no
one else's rules. If you long to find God, to find your
own divinity, you will be called upon to follow your
own rules because you are unique and vast and powerful, and within you lies a totally perfect rhythm
and way to go about your life. If you would listen to
it! Listen to your deep self.

Tap your own deepest truth and put that into action.

You may find that you will take one ritual from one path, and one from another and none from another and so be it! You hold your own path inside of you. What you do, day by day IS your path. Your path and your life are not separate. Everyone's path is different. Your ego has come to believe that you must be like everybody else, and then it struggles to convince itself that you are better than everybody else! The ego says to keep following the rules and one day you will find enlightenment.

Enlightenment is within you Now.

Your ego loses out by this truth, but it is the truth! Your ego is not the truth and be grateful for that. Your ego feels afraid of surrendering to the higher self and it will do what it may to keep you trapped. Egos do not make for happiness. If you really want to know God, then listen to your deep self! Try it for a year or two, and see if there is not a very deep change within you. You are the Light! You are beautiful, powerful and wise! Claim that truth and be free.

Perhaps one of the most distinct aspects of a loving being is that they have come to terms with the shadow within themselves. Understand that this world is a mirror.

Everyone you encounter is a reflection of some part of you.

That is why certain media figures or certain friends of yours are idolized, immortalized and idealized or disliked and rejected. When you see a facet of another that you deeply love, it is a reflection of that facet in yourself, whether it is developed or not. When you see a facet of another being that you dislike, you dislike that facet of your own being whether it is prominent or not. Before you can truly love all others, you must come to terms with ALL of the parts of your wholeness, and that includes the dark-ness — the shadow.

The human condition involves the polarity of both Yin and Yang, feminine and masculine, joy and sorrow, up and down and this must be em-braced by your inner depths in order to see that you cannot judge another when you are just as they are. You hold all aspects of human moods, emotions, thoughts and desires inside of you. It is very helpful to embrace these aspects, all of them and come to terms with them if you are serious about allowing your wholeness to emerge. An enlightened one is so loving because they have embraced these parts in themselves, and are no longer taken off center by the mirror reflection others provide. They no longer have an unaccepted shadow. And then they see THROUGH all facets of humanness and into the Divine, into the unnameable, the Creator of all. They see that you can mold clay into a hero or a villain but it is all the same clay! They see that the darkness doesn't need to be sorted through, analyzed or dwelled upon — that is mental imbalance — it simply needs to be acknowledged, held and loved.

First comes the acceptance of the parts of your wholeness and then comes bliss — the bliss that says "You are Me, I am You. Your darkness is My own, your Beauty is My own, and so be it!" Then every-where you go, you are the Wholeness, you are giving, you are sensitive to all of your brothers and sisters, and that is joy and the Light eternal.

*You are the Light of Lights,
the endless Rainbow of Dawn,
streaming forth.*

CHAPTER NINE
ENLIGHTENMENT
IS YOU

Enlightenment is you, dancing to the timeless essence.

To discover what is true and timeless in yourself and in your world, use the beauty — the timeless part of yourself. Move beyond thought and into the stillness, into giving over your entire being, body and mind, to the stillness. Thus arises the flame of the heart, the softness of love and of selfless action as it slips gently into your life.

The silence is the spaciousness of a clear mind, the expansiveness and joy of an open heart, a deep compassion and a sincerity towards all beings. The silence is a deep connection with nature and a quality of sharing and of listening. Listening without thinking of what you will say when the other is finished.

Listen and you will hear the silence.

An instant benediction comes from inner stillness. Cutting through into now — into what is. You know your true Self by being in the now, with whatever is going on within and without. When you truly know yourself, you know all others; you walk without fear. You are never afraid of that which you deeply know.

When you are sincere, doors will open. When you believe, magic happens. You are the rain dancer, the story spinner, the dream weaver. Weave your dreams well and they will be heard for many miles. Share your dreams softly and they will be heard for many moons. Become as the song of the midnight sun, the Light from within to show the way. Share the truth of goodness. Love arises when you are full of the stillness and silence within.

The power to discover your Self lies within.

ENLIGHTENMENT IS YOU

When one says that they are searching for the timeless Self, this implies becoming — today I do not have it but tomorrow, if I go to the right place, I may find it. You may put the object of your search outside of yourself and place your enlightenment at the mercy of an external force — not within your own immediate grasp. You may depend upon an authority outside yourself to tell you whether or not you have reached the state of enlightenment. If you have given the power of your own authority away to some other, take it gently back.

Another cannot possibly know for you. Enlightenment is immediate and it is a journey — a wondrous, magical journey. It is whole and it is all of the parts — the intricate, amazing parts. It is a swirling, warm, magical comforting power. When you trust that all is working itself out in a perfect, Divine way and you are not attached to those things which you believe have made you feel good or bad, then the deep knowingness is yours.

You are the actor or actress, director and stuntperson of your life, sustained by the omniscient Spiritual Source.

The movement and energy of searching can be transformed into one of having and knowing the moment you perceive yourself and the world around you with openness, safety, trust and love and you realize that you give meaning to the things that move in and out of your life.

You are an infinite being, filled and flowing with powerful Infinite energy. You hold the key to all of your dreams.

See yourself as
eternally beautiful,
for you are.

You are a majestic book, a beautiful and fascinating tale. Read yourself. Empower your world and feel the warmth shining brilliantly back at you. Dance your unique dance of Life. Share your joy and your laughter. God bless you.

Floating upon the deep waters
of the Infinite Sunrise Within
is your Wholeness.

Elizabeth Joy is an author, an artist, and a teacher. She brings to her work a rich background of metaphysics and spirituality. Elizabeth believes that within each person lies infinite love, wisdom, inspiration and joy, and that these gifts are expressed when each person chooses to awaken to them. Her books and tapes reflect this belief.

Other books by Elizabeth Joy:

AWAKENING
Practical Spirituality

GAYLORD
FG